INDiE AUTHOR MAGAZINE

HELLO AND WELCOME!

I'm Indie Annie, and I'm thrilled you're reading this gorgeous full-color version of IAM. Did you know that you can also access all the information, education, and inspiration in our app? It's available on both the iOS App Store and Google Play. And for those that prefer to listen to me read articles, you can pop over to Spotify or our website. Happy Reading!

X

IndieAuthorMagazine.com

Download on the
App Store

GET IT ON
Google Play

Spotify

MARKET RESEARCH

22

BOOK INFLUENCERS HELP TURN A NEW PAGE IN PUBLISHING

28

THE INDIE AUTHOR'S RECIPE FOR CROSS-GENRE SUCCESS

34

MARKETING 101

Ready to Boost Your Book Sales? School's in Session

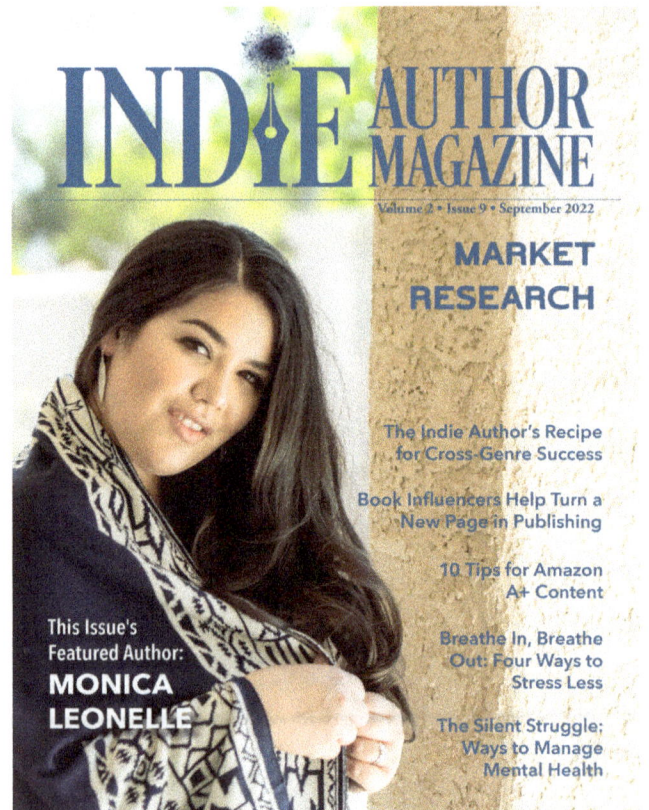

ON THE COVER

INDIE AUTHOR MAGAZINE

PUBLISHER
Chelle Honiker

CREATIVE DIRECTOR
Alice Briggs

EDITOR IN CHIEF
Nicole Schroeder

COPY EDITOR
Lisa Thompson

WRITERS
Angela Archer
Elaine Bateman
Patricia Carr
Bradley Charbonneau
Laurel Decher
Fatima Fayez
Gill Fernley
Greg Fishbone
Chrishaun Keller-Hanna
Jac Harmon
Marion Hermannsen
Natalie Hobbs

WRITERS
Kasia Lasinska
Megan Linski-Fox
Bre Lockhart
Sìne Màiri MacDougall
Angie Martin
Merri Maywether
Susan Odev
Jenn Mitchell
Clare Sager
Nicole Schroeder
Emilia Zeeland

PUBLISHER
Athenia Creative
6820 Apus Dr.
Sparks, NV, 89436 USA
775.298.1925

ISSN 2768-7880 (online)–ISSN 2768-7872 (print)

From the Publisher

TO CHANGE OR NOT TO CHANGE

I've been a bit of a process improvement nerd since my days with a company that was chasing the illustrious Malcolm Baldrige National Quality Award. The award is the nation's highest presidential honor for performance excellence.

Our strategy for winning included looking at every department of a large travel management company with a fine tooth comb and documenting the minute-by-minute actions of each team member for an entire month.

Once we had that data, we then analyzed how to optimize operations with a mind-numbing degree of specificity and precision, which would then translate to time and money savings—and that award.

I was trained to measure everything and to look for improvements in mundane tasks, from how long it took to travel to the printer to how we could end calls faster so our team could take another call.

We all hated the minutiae of tracking and tracking our every move. And making changes was even more painful.

Why fix it if it ain't broke?

I've been trained to believe that change just for the sake of change is usually a disaster. It's important to have data to back up proposed changes.

But on the other side of that is "analysis paralysis," where you can overthink something and kill any potential due to indecision.

As indie authors, time is money. We only have ourselves to rely on for decisions—and that's a good thing. But I see too many authors make decisions based on their gut or because something didn't feel like it was working. Your ads aren't converting? What's the data say? Maybe your keywords are off. Book not selling? Look at the data. Perhaps your cover isn't what others in your genre look like.

Gather the data. Make an informed decision. Chase your own quality award.

To Your Success,
Chelle
Publisher
Indie Author Magazine

From the Editor

A few weeks ago, I spent an afternoon shopping for school supplies with my younger sister. She'll be a freshman in college this year, attending the same university I did, and while I'm helping her prepare—showing her around campus, explaining how the bus system works and where to buy textbooks—I can't help but feel nostalgic.

As a kid, I always secretly loved heading back to school. I would spend the last few weeks in August looking forward to Meet the Teacher Night and comparing schedules with my friends, making sure we at least shared the same lunch period. Years later, I still get excited when I see ads for all the notebooks, planners, and pens going on sale—though to be honest, what writer doesn't? For me, the school year always meant organized notes, interesting lectures, and poring over books I wouldn't normally think to read. It meant late-night study sessions and stress before an exam, but it also meant researching essay topics I didn't realize I was passionate about and the tired relief I'd feel when I'd finally turn in a project.

Our stories this month show how indie publishing can recreate those same memories. Plenty of us wile away the nights doing research for our books or reading about new marketing trends, like serialized fiction or transmedia. We work to create eye-catching designs with our Amazon A+ Content, just like the posters we made for in-class presentations. We build out schedules and set ourselves deadlines, and we're no strangers to the library or the local coffee shops. We're constantly reading, writing, editing, and learning, and when it's all said and done, we hold our finished projects and feel that same tired relief tenfold.

So ready your notebooks, and sharpen your pencils. Class is starting—and yes, there will be homework.

Nicole Schroeder
Editor in Chief
Indie Author Magazine

Chasing the Unicorn

YOUR BEST BOOK IS ALWAYS YET TO COME

What is the best story you ever wrote?

My answer will always be the next one. I have those that are good, and those I consider the best so far, but better lies ahead.

Otherwise, this would be a tough business. It would be soul crushing to think that I'd never write a book that was as good as one I've already written.

And published.

The unicorn is ahead, even if lightning has struck, and you've already realized immense success. That's also a unicorn. Too much success too soon and the authors won't know what they did right. They won't be able to replicate it. I've seen that too many times. The best book was first, and by book five, they are fading from memory.

The price of success comes at a cost when the best book is first and not last.

The magnum opus comes as a culmination to a career, not its opening act.

Have you learned nothing with each new book? I know you have learned something. You know you have. Then how could you not spin a tighter tale, deliver a greater impact with new words?

Life is a journey of continuous improvement. Too often, we compare our first efforts against another's magnum opus. You shouldn't, and you can't. We progress through life, and we progress through our careers.

The best is the sum total of what we've learned from our experiences. That's called wisdom. And we're still learning. Every day.

Because the best is yet to come. ∎

Craig Martelle

Dear Indie Annie,

I have a great idea, or at least I think it is, for a series of books that would be a mash-up of a couple of other famous series. I wouldn't use the same characters or world, but the plots would be somewhat similar. But then I wonder if I shouldn't bother because it's been done before. Should I write my idea or try to find something completely original?

Mash-up in Mainz

DEAR MASH-UP,

How thrilling it is to hear from you. I love your question. No, really, I do because this dilemma is one that has faced writers since we first put pen to paper or even chisel to stone.

As our ancestors gathered around open fires telling epic sagas of heroines battling dragons, do we think they cared if their history borrowed themes, tropes, or plotlines from other legends? Obviously, we can't answer that question for sure, but I am pretty certain that the answer is a flat no. In fact, I am going to stick my blue-silk-scarfed neck out here and suggest that they welcomed the opportunity to improve their stories with outside influences.

The term "mash-up," according to the Oxford English Dictionary, is a "mixture or fusion of disparate elements." Although the entry states it is a term that was rarely used until the twentieth century, there is at least one reference to a "mash-up" in 1859. The reference is from Boucicault's *Octoroon,* which has a line that goes, "He don't understand; he speaks a mash up of Indian, French, and Mexican."

I adore that line because it encapsulates exactly what a mash-up really is. A mash-up is evolution.

A mash-up is how we, as humans, have developed—through mixing up language and ideas. The term might be modern, but the concept is as old as time.

Homo sapiens have been on this planet for around two hundred thousand years. Therefore, as a species, we have been talking and sharing and telling stories for millennia. Do you really think you can come up with a story that is completely unique? Seems pretty arrogant to me to think that you can.

I don't like to quote chapter and verse to anyone, but in this case, all I will say is Ecclesiastes 1:9: "The thing that

hath been, it is that which shall be; and that which is done is that which shall be done: and there is no new thing under the sun." (King James Bible)

So take a leaf out of George Lucas's playbook, a well-worn story arc, e.g., the hero's journey. Add in some proven tropes—in his case, good versus evil as a Western-style showdown, right down to the goodies and baddies in white and black outfits. And set the saga in a galaxy far, far away. I could spend many columns unpacking all the ideas Lucas adapted from classical storytelling, folklore, and popular culture, but plenty of books and online fora have already done that much better than I.

And it's not just Star Wars. Consider how the Harry Potter series took ancient myths and weaved them into a wizarding world—and may or may not have stolen several ideas from the Lord of the Rings or even Malory Towers! Or how *West Side Story* is a revamped musical version of Shakespeare's *Romeo and Juliet*. And we all know good ole Shakespeare himself wasn't afraid of a mash-up of his own. He found inspiration in Greek and Roman legends and contemporary books and plays. In turn, Shakespeare's work inspired others. Aldous Huxley's *Brave New World*

is modeled on Shakespeare's *The Tempest. Macbeth* inspired *The Talented Mr. Ripley* by Patricia Highsmith. Frederick Forsyth's *The Dogs of War* has a lot in common with the bard's version of the life of Julius Caesar. The list goes on and on.

The thing is, the greatest stories speak to us of the human condition, of the trials and challenges, hopes and dreams of our kind. We all want to see the hero emerge victorious at the end of their quest, whether that is to return a ring to the fiery pits of hell or return a faulty toaster. We also want things to work out for the cute couple who met by chance on the station platform, in the coffee shop, or in the gladiatorial training academy of some post-apocalyptic world. And we all want the baddie to come to a sticky end. My favorite is the truck of manure emptying its contents over the bully Biff and his convertible in *Back to the Future*, but you may prefer seeing your MC's nemesis being blown apart by the last shot from a homemade catapult or by falling on their own laser sword.

So, dear friend, you are following along a path well trodden by other writers, past and present. Do not be afraid. Mash away.

Happy writing,
Indie Annie

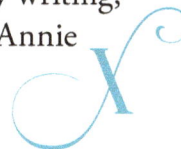

10 TIPS FOR
AMAZON A+ CONTENT

Since early 2021, indie authors have had the ability to create Amazon A+ Content to help promote their books. This bonus content on a book's product page had already been available for traditional publishing houses for some time and had proven its merit—in 2015, during a ninety-day study of 134,000 products, Amazon found that A+ Content increased sales (depending on content quality, product price, and product category) 3 to 10 percent. The simple formats and design elements give your potential reader an additional glimpse into you, the author, as well as your book, and can go above and beyond the traditional written description.

Your first reactions may be one of either extreme: "Yay! More pretties!" or "Oh, no, not something else to do!" But carefully consider if and how this type of expanded content on your book's pages may benefit your sales. Amazon prominently displays A+ Content on product detail pages, and on mobile devices, it may appear before the description for some users. Keep that in mind as you are deciding what type of content you use, as well as the message you're sending with your content. Professional images and copy will be key and will help your A+ Content earn an A+ from readers as expressed in clicks of the "Buy Now" button.

1 KNOW THE MARKETPLACES

A+ Content is not available on all Amazon marketplaces, but it is available at the time of writing in these fifteen countries: Canada, the United States, Australia, Brazil, Mexico, the United Kingdom, Germany, Spain, France, India, Italy, the Netherlands, Poland, Sweden, and Japan. If your book is available in multiple marketplaces and the reader has your language as their preference, then Amazon will duplicate your content as a draft across all applicable marketplaces, so you can easily replicate your efforts. English A+ Content will be available in the United States, United Kingdom, and India, as well as for English speakers elsewhere. Amazon won't automatically publish to all the applicable platforms, but they will duplicate your content as a draft, which you can edit and then approve.

② PREORDERS AND REVIEWS NEED NOT APPLY

A+ Content is only available for live titles, not preorders. You also may not use quotes from individuals, customers, or private people. You can have up to four endorsements from well-known publications or public figures, and you also must document the source. Also not allowed are symbols, special characters, contact information, website links, low-quality images, buzzwords like "cutting-edge," and warranties or guarantees.

③ THINK FORMATS AND SERIES

If your book is in a series, you can create A+ Content for the series and apply that same A+ Content to all the ASINs, Amazon's unique product identification numbers, that apply.

Pro Tip: If hiring a designer, thinking in terms of the series can save you money as well as excite readers about other titles in your series. Also, don't forget to add the ASINs of paperback, hardcover, and/or audio versions as well. Your A+ Content will work equally well there.

④ START HERE

Add A+ Content from the KDP Marketing page. Click on the "Promote and Advertise" button, and scroll down on the next page, choose your marketplace, and click "Manage A+ Content." Also on that page are three helpful articles from Amazon to ensure that your content complies with their guidelines and can be served. Once there, you'll be able to choose your modules, add content, and submit for review.

⑤ SELECT THE RIGHT MODULES

Amazon provides a large list of modules to choose from when creating your content, allowing you to select a layout for the information you want to display. Module options include: Company Logo, Comparison Chart, Four Image & Text, Four Image/Text Quadrant, Image and Dark Text Overlay, Image and Light Text Overlay, Image Header with Text, Multiple Image Module A, Product Description Text, Single Image and Highlights, Single Image and Sidebar, Single Image and Specs Details, Single Left Image, Single Right Image, Technical Specifications, Text, and Three Images and Text.

Pro Tip: Choose modules wisely. Some authors have found that you can only add up to five modules, though Amazon doesn't outline this in its guidelines.

⑥ CONTENT IS KING AND QUEEN

Remember that A+ Content is prime real estate on your page for advertising your book. Professional images consistent with your branding are a must, as is strong copywriting. Be clear and consistent so as not to confuse your reader.

Pro Tip: A confused mind doesn't buy, so take some time to carefully construct your content, and make your message crystal clear before you upload it for the best results.

7 BRAINSTORM CONTENT IDEAS

Kindlepreneur's Jason Hamilton offers several ideas for making the most of your content space. Use this as additional author page space, he suggests, or create photo ads. A timeline can be especially helpful in a shared universe or overlapping series. Hamilton also suggests creating an infographic, comparing all your series, using the tech specs to outline your world-building facts, or designing a character carousel. You can find more on these ideas to spark your own creativity here: https://kindlepreneur.com/amazon-a-content.

Pro Tip: Dimensions are 600 x 180 pixels per inch (ppi) for a "standard company logo" module, 970 x 300 ppi for the "standard image with text overlay" module, and 300 x 300 ppi for the "standard three images" module.

8 A+ CONTENT INCREASES SALES

As we mentioned above, Amazon demonstrated that A+ Content increased sales throughout their store. This isn't a guarantee that it will do the same for your books but is worth considering. Testing A+ Content on your most popular book or series may be the best way forward to see if it works for your readers and is worth the extra effort. If your data shows that sales have increased, you can then create the content on all your titles.

Pro Tip: You are not your reader. Many authors say they personally dislike A+ Content, so they won't try it. This is a common advertising fallacy. Your readers may not respond in ways you personally would. The only way to know is to try it and see. Amazon Ads will give you the stats you need for a before and after comparison as long as you keep all other factors constant.

Pro Tip: If you have many titles and series, work in descending order of popularity one or a few at a time so you don't get overwhelmed or derail your writing and publishing progress.

9 AMAZON LOG-IN CREDENTIALS WORK FOR EVERY MARKETPLACE

This tip isn't specific to A+ Content, but as this might be the first time you'll be logging into another marketplace's dashboard, no, you don't need new log-in information. Your credentials work platform wide.

10 DON'T REINVENT THE WHEEL

Check out best sellers in your categories and genre, and see what's working well for them. Don't copy exactly what they're doing, but note the types of modules they are using and how you can adapt similar modules to your own book.

Pro Tip: The split-and-stacked image seems popular in many genres. To achieve the look, create one image at 970 x 900 ppi and crop it into three 970 x 300 ppi images. Then, use the "standard image with text overlay" module—just upload the image without adding text.

If you are looking for A+ book sales, Amazon A+ Content might be just what you need to make the grade. ■

Alice Briggs

The Woman with a Read on the Future

HOW MONICA LEONELLE'S TECH BACKGROUND KICK-STARTED INDIE PUBLISHING SUCCESS

As a *USA Today* best-selling author and with over fifty books to her credit, Monica Leonelle has earned her reputation as a productive novelist. She shares the title with one of her two nonfiction series for authors. She writes quickly and publishes often.

She's also one of the most marketing-savvy authors in the business with a deep understanding of how to write persuasive copy and get her books in the hands of readers. This one-two punch makes her an unmitigated success; she can write and market like some can walk and chew gum.

BIG TECH BEGINNINGS

Leonelle started her career as a software engineer, spending years in "Big Tech" before earning her MBA and then taking executive positions in marketing at startup companies. Her author career started in 2009. Initially, Leonelle's career goals included public speaking, she says, and in her mind, publishing was the thing she needed to do "to get to the other thing." Her first book was about social media and how companies could utilize it. At the time, Twitter was just a few months old, and Instagram didn't yet exist.

That first book sparked an epiphany.

The technical aspect of self-publishing wasn't as easy in 2009 as it is today, but even then, Leonelle could already see the upside to self-publishing. Social media was evolving quickly, enough so that it made little sense to go through the process of traditional publishing with its longer lead times. Had she waited for a traditional deal like some others she knew, the content in her book would probably have been outdated.

But more importantly, she enjoyed it. "I just got really hooked on publishing books," she says. "That was not the goal."

Leonelle continued to work at tech startups for a couple of years after she published her nonfiction book, but she also continued to write. In 2011, she published her first work of fiction.

Something clicked. "Until then, I had been looking for 'my thing,' like my one thing—the career I knew I could invest in forever. And I had tried software, and then I had tried marketing," she says. "And every single time I switched [careers], I was like, 'Okay, I can see that I'm getting closer, but it's not the thing.' And then finally with books, I was like, 'This is the thing.' And I had been searching for it for seven or eight years, and then it was there."

From 2010 to 2014, she wrote fiction while she freelanced full time. She wrote Steamy Contemporary Romance under a pen name but finally shut it down because she "didn't have the passion for it, which I think is needed in this industry."

She says the lessons she learned were invaluable to her future success. "I had learned to write really fast from freelancing and from fiction. And I learned dictation. I wrote an article about [dictation], and then it was like ten thousand words. And I kept getting questions."

From that article and the questions she was asked, she expanded the article to forty thousand words and published it on Amazon for ninety-nine cents. She says the cover was the "worst in the world," and she had no expectations for success.

Nonetheless, success happened. Leonelle sold over twenty thousand copies and later turned that book into a series with two new books: *The 8-Minute Writing Habit* and *Dictate Your Book*. She eventually decided the books' popularity came from the questions they answered for her readers. "That's something I've learned about nonfiction," she says. "It wasn't based on something that I wanted to talk about. It was based on something that other people wanted to talk about."

EXPANDING THE UNIVERSE

After going full time, Leonelle's next focus was to look for ways to expand beyond publishing solely on Amazon. She says that while it makes sense, other revenue opportunities exist for authors.

She had been online friends with *USA Today* best-selling author, publisher, and speaker Russell Nohelty for years when she learned he was looking for someone to take over his content, books, and courses.

They signed a publishing agreement in 2020. In March 2021, Leonelle approached him with an idea to use his content to create a new five-book series. He was inspired, and they teamed up and planned a sixteen-book series called *Book Sales Supercharged* with a staggered release schedule over the next year. Each book explains one facet of a specific sales strategy: how authors can maximize sales through print copies, by using Facebook, by creating translations and audiobooks, by releasing via Apple Books, and by launching on Kickstarter.

"We did not intend to start a company together," she says. "We did not intend to start a Kickstarter course together. I hadn't met him in person actually until very recently. We were basically already almost business partners by the time I met him, which is weird."

KICKING OFF KICKSTARTER

One of the books in that series, *Get Your Book Selling on Kickstarter*, was based on the campaigns Nohelty had been running for his own books over the last couple of years.

"Russell had done the work, and we had proven the concept ourselves," she says. All that was left was to share it with other indie authors.

In November 2021, the two of them ran a Kickstarter campaign. As part of the campaign, they planned to release the book in July 2022.

"It was just kind of this funny, very meta thing that we were like, it'll be a fun promotion. And then [Nohelty] was like, we have to hit ten thousand [dollars] on this, or else it looks stupid."

Leonelle wondered about the goal since she hadn't yet run a campaign herself. She needn't have worried. The pair's campaign ended with over twenty thousand dollars in pledges.

Then, a few months later, author Brandon Sanderson made Kickstarter history in March 2022 with his campaign, raising more than forty-one million dollars to publish four new books—half of that in the first seventy-two hours alone. "The whole publishing community was like, 'Wait, what? What's Kickstarter?'" Leonelle says. "And Russell was like, 'You've got to publish the e-book,' because we hadn't even put the e-book out."

They took advantage of the zeitgeist of Sanderson's wave of publicity and created a course with students from many genres. This gave the duo added data they could use to update the book and create a podcast to share case studies from their students.

"The highest campaign was about forty thousand dollars. The lowest is a thousand or something," she says. "Most of them are fiction authors. Most of them are first-time Kickstarter authors. I think almost everybody has raised over a thousand at this point, as far as I know. And as far as I know, everybody has funded."

Leonelle suggests that the spillover from Brandon Sanderson's popular Kickstarter campaign is helping other indie authors. "I think that's why Kickstarter is having its moment—because of attention arbitrage."

SEEING THE FUTURE

Leonelle's old stomping grounds within the technology and marketing industries offer her a unique perspective on the business side of publishing. She can spot trends before they're visible to others—and she's not hesitant to share them.

"I believe that publishing has become a 'Big Tech' battleground," Leonelle says. "And you can see that even though authors are still a bit

Amazon focused, Amazon is just one of the big players in the publishing space right now. Google, for example—they're very interested in audiobooks."

She says indie authors should pay attention to the trends in audiobooks. Right now, audiobooks are less than 5 percent of the market, and e-books were once less than 5 percent as well.

"As audiobooks grow, 'Big Tech' is coming back around again to the little indie publishing space, trying to win market share. Spotify is making really big moves in audiobooks right now. Google Play Books is making huge moves in audiobooks with its AI narration, Apple Books also."

She continues, pointing out that Google, Apple, and Spotify dominate the mobile distribution channel and can get audiobooks and podcasts in the hands of most device owners globally.

membership programs: the Go Wide, Grow Wide *Incubator* and the Kickstarter Accelerator.

From a creative perspective, she's ready to write fiction again after taking a break in 2019. "Creatively, I feel like there are seasons for myself," she says. "I realized that I really just want to make sure that my fiction backlist is in really good shape. I really want to get all of those rewrites done, get books republished, get new books out, and finish up series."

With Leonelle's penchant for productivity, give her a weekend to whip it into shape.

Find out more about Monica Leonelle at KickstartYourNovel.com or GoWideGrowWide.com. ■

Chelle Honiker

WHAT'S NEXT?

Like most serial entrepreneurs, Leonelle's continually asking herself, "What's next?" She and Nohelty have established two author

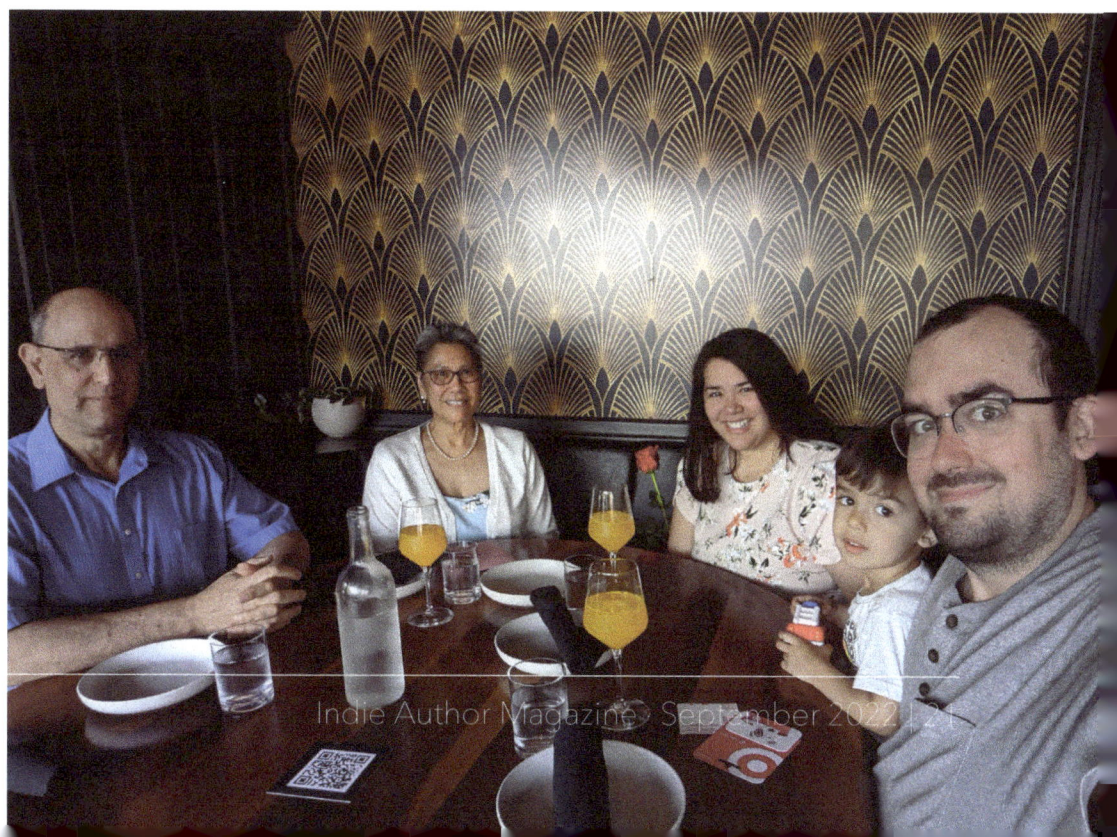

Book Influencers Help Turn a New Page in Publishing

Nestled in her New England home, independent bookseller Kaitee Yaeko Tredway spends time each week arranging stacks of books and displaying them against a variety of backgrounds. She snaps several photos and writes out creative captions to pair with each, then decides when they'll publish. Sometimes, she makes an appearance in front of the camera too, posing with a recent read or filming and editing a ninety-second video if she thinks she can find a creative spin on a trend or make it fit within her niche.

Kaitee Yaeko Tredway works as an independent bookseller by day, but even in her free time, she's introducing readers to new authors and stories through Bookstagram.

Tredway, the face behind the Instagram account @kaiteeyaeko.writes, is part of a corner of social media that has been dominated by readers and book lovers in recent years. Especially during the pandemic shutdowns of 2020, reading-centered accounts exploded in number and popularity across YouTube, Instagram, Twitter, and TikTok, leading to massive spikes in book sales. In 2021, readers bought more than 825 million print books, according to NPD BookScan (https://npd.com), an industry analytics tracker. The number is the highest on record since the organization began tracking data in 2004 and came on the heels of a similar year of growth for the industry in 2020.

The boost in sales is felt even more acutely by authors whose works have gone viral. Madeline Miller's *The Song of Achilles* was traditionally published in 2012 with a print run of twenty thousand units; in July of this year, according to the *New York Times*, the book's publisher reported selling two million copies across all formats.

In some cases, the shift has extended to authors from diverse backgrounds or those outside the traditionally popular sphere, such as self-published authors or those writing in niche genres. With the number of online literary enthusiasts growing, the trend may suggest a leveling playing field in the world of book marketing and offer further proof of just how much influence these online reading communities have on the publishing world.

queer_bookwyrm

Liked by **kaiteeyaeko.writes** and **405 others**
queer_bookwyrm 🏳️‍🌈 Happy Friday, Bookwyrms! 🐛
🏳️‍⚧️

Cheyenne Robinson-Bauman joined Books-tagram while working from home to connect with other book lovers and discover new books.

A PANDEMIC BOOK CLUB OF SORTS

For Cheyenne Robinson-Bauman, who manages the Instagram account @queer_bookwyrm, being part of "Bookstagram"—bookish Instagram—has served as an introduction to indie authors, as well as an opportunity to introduce readers to more books by diverse authors.

"Before [Bookstagram], I couldn't name an indie author or even know where to find them," they write. "I think [Bookstagram] has kind of given indie authors and self-published authors more legitimacy and has helped their reach. Unfortunately, I think it has also negatively impacted traditional publishing in the way that popular authors only get more popular and the others fall to the wayside."

Robinson-Bauman began their account in September 2020 after they began working from home, only one month before Tredway created hers. Tredway, on the other hand, started her account as a way to market book-related cross-stitch projects she was selling through Etsy—her own "pandemic project," she says. As time went on, she found herself posting less about her bookish artwork and more about the books themselves.

Both agree the community they've discovered—and helped grow—has been one of the better parts of their platforms. "Social media can be a mixed bag at times with the negativity on high, but I've only had positive experiences with the other accounts I follow," Robinson-Bauman writes. "I've also made some great friends from all over the world." In their two years on Instagram, both Robinson-Bauman's and Tredway's accounts have garnered audiences of more than six thousand members strong.

"My favorite thing is finding people who read books in the same way that I do—the people who love a book enough to not judge that you have five copies and who want to live inside the characters the way you do, so they go and they put together a cosplay," Tredway says. But she also enjoys supporting and promoting her favorite authors, "especially because a lot of the books I love don't necessarily get the mainstream attention the way some of the big authors do."

The authors she's referencing include many women, people of color, and LGBTQ+-identifying people—authors regularly featured on Robinson-Bauman's account as well. Both Tredway, as a queer, biracial Asian woman, and Robinson-Bauman, as someone who is queer, nonbinary, and biracial, find themselves drawn to diverse stories that reflect their identities and present new experiences. But that doesn't mean every part of book social media is as inclusive, Tredway says. In other corners of Bookstagram, she's seen people post photos of books by marginalized authors yet never get around to reading them, and as often as Twitter or TikTok posts have boosted authors' names for great reasons, she also can name authors who have suffered intense scrutiny or criticism.

Robinson-Bauman agrees. "I see a lot of people post a certain book during an awareness week or during pride month, but [they] have rarely read those books," they write. Although they believe social media's influence has helped boost diverse representation in some ways, they believe the industry as a whole "still has a long way to go."

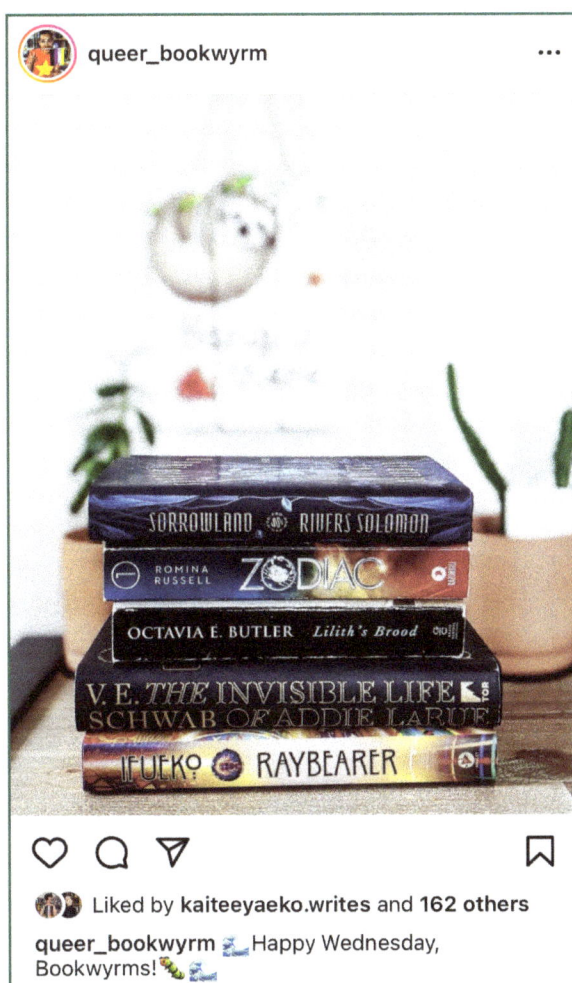

Robinson-Bauman tends to read more YA, Sci-Fi, and Fantasy books. "You won't find many thrillers or romance on my page," they write.

THE INFLUENCE EXTENDS TO INDIES

Importantly, the indie author sphere is one such area where Robinson-Bauman believes book influencers are helping increase representation and, considering the bias and discrimination they believe exists among traditional publishers, truly shape the industry.

Tredway admits she isn't as familiar with books by indie authors. "I'm going to be very frank about it—part of that is that I don't see a lot of authors of color in the indie sphere on Bookstagram." She knows they exist, she says, but she hasn't taken the time to look for them and hasn't come across them in her Bookstagram feed. Still, she has witnessed the potential of partnerships between indie authors and book influencers thanks to a series of cosplay collaborations between indie authors and a friend of hers on Bookstagram under the handle @live_1000_lives.

"Since January, she has integrated into her cosplay three characters at this point from new releases of indie authors," she says. The collaborations were successful at boosting the authors and promoting their work, especially because their genres aligned well, she says. She thinks that kind of compatibility can help other indie authors establish a relationship with book influencers and grow alongside them. "As soon as you find the people who read books that you like, you find people who are going to like to read the book that you write," she says.

Most of what Tredway reads and shares on Bookstagram is written by authors in marginalized communities. "Once I found stories that centered characters who looked like me, loved like me, and struggled with similar questions of identity, I couldn't get enough," she writes.

Rather than using the platform strictly as a marketing tool, she encourages authors to post about other books they enjoy and truly engage with the community. "As an author, finding your niche in that, that's tied directly to your age group and your genre, and then sticking your fingers into the community there ... is a way that Bookstagram can actually work for you without it being a huge marketing slog," Tredway says.

"Get to know your community, and who knows what collaborations might grow out of that," she adds.

Robinson-Bauman also emphasizes the relationship between indie authors and reading personalities. They encourage those wanting to promote their work to reach out to content creators. "Bookstagrammers are typically really supportive people. Sometimes, you can even make great friends that will become critique partners, beta readers, editors, and ARC street teams. Some of my best friends on Instagram are indie authors. ... Go to where the readers are."

A growing number of those readers seem to be found on social media—all it takes is a search for the proper hashtag. ■

Nicole Schroeder

The Indie Author's Recipe for Cross-Genre Success

You've committed what is considered the grave sin of indie publishing—you've written a book that doesn't cleanly fit into any specific genre or category. Hosts of fellow writers would tell you to immediately abandon the project because attempting to market or, heaven forbid, sell a novel with no easily identifiable audience is doomed to fail in the current write-to-market atmosphere.

But a cross-genre book doesn't need to spell the death of your writing career. You can sell that ugly duckling and possibly turn it into a swan that'll deliver a host of new fans and meet sales goals. Will it be more difficult than selling a highly packaged piece of genre fiction? Perhaps, but why did we become indie authors if not to embrace challenges and explore new frontiers?

STEP 1: UNDERSTAND CRAFT

When writing cross-genre fiction, though the idea may be unique, the aspects of crafting story remain the same.

Joseph Lallo is a full-time author and a co-host of the podcast Six Figure Authors. He has made a career out of writing cross-genre series, most particularly his Book of Deacon series, a High Fantasy saga that features Sci-Fi elements due to the advanced technical magic system within the books. His other works include the Free-Wrench series, which he describes as Steampunk with Fantasy elements.

"Every genre is defined by a handful of things. A book becomes cross-genre when you combine the rules of two different genres," Lallo says. "Look at the elements of genre that are going to work best for your story. Establish the rules and start defining your system. You want the story to make sense and be consistent. The rules of writing and creating a book do not change."

A strong plot and compelling characters can make or break a cross-genre series. In order to achieve a truly marketable product, you must have both, no matter what genre you're writing.

"You have to have the fundamentals in place," Lallo says. "Readers want something that's familiar to them. The novelty of a book can be super interesting, but what gets people to finish a book and read the next one is how good the book is, not how good the idea is."

STEP 2: PICK A LANE

All cross-genre books have to start somewhere, and that means determining exactly what your book is, even if it turns out to be a mishmash of everything. To market correctly, you must analyze which genre your book is closest to.

"Look at the category the book leans stronger toward and the broadest category with the readers who will accept the most variation," Lallo says.

Take, for example, a Historical Fantasy with Dystopian elements and a bit of Romance thrown in. At first glance, this book could fit into a number of categories. But upon analysis, the Historical Fantasy aspect might make up around 70 percent of the book while the Dystopian parts make up about 20 percent and the Romance only 10 percent. In this case, you would market the book as a Historical Fantasy and label the other two categories as subgenres.

Assigning your book a subgenre, or a secondary category, can serve as an alternate way of marketing to a different audience. In this way, you're demonstrating to your audience that you primarily see your work as a Historical Fantasy, but readers who enjoy Historical Fantasy along with Dystopian and Romance will find it entertaining. The idea is to market toward one overall audience segment, then find readers who would also enjoy the subgenres in the book, instead of working the other way around.

Beta readers can be highly helpful in this regard. Ask a group of readers to read the novel before publication and fill out a questionnaire once they've completed the novel to help you categorize your book correctly. Include questions like:

If you had to put this book into one category at the bookstore, what category would that be?

If you couldn't put this book into the category you mentioned above, what other section would you expect to find it in?

What is the first word that pops into your head when asked what this novel is about?

If you had to compare this book to one or two other titles that you already know about, what would you say it is similar to?

If you were recommending this book to a friend, how would you describe the plot and/or characters in a few sentences?

STEP 3: NAIL YOUR PACKAGING

Branding a cross-genre book is of exceptional importance, as it gives readers expectations on the kind of reading experience they'll have while enjoying your book. Because of this, the cover art and marketing copy—the reader's first connection with your book—must be on point in order to make the novel an easier sell.

"Find the closest genre to your book that people understand," Lallo says. "The blurb and cover need to be solid so people can make an educated decision."

STEP 4: EXPERIMENT WITH MARKETING STRATEGIES

At its forefront, marketing a cross-genre book should be a simple matter, much like the marketing of an on-genre product.

"The less you have to educate your reader during the marketing process, the better," Lallo says. "Market the book as one genre with elements of another genre. Don't make your readers solve a puzzle, trying to figure out what the book is."

When considering advertising, such as social media ads or newsletter marketing, Lallo says it's important to first understand the audience for your ads—the website users, their ages, and their buying habits. Still, one marketing strategy stands true overall.

"Return on word-of-mouth is through the roof. Make people aware, through back matter or social media, if they like the book to tell their friends, and that this is one way they can help the author," Lallo says.

The best tactic an author can use to promote their work, however, is by showing the world just how much passion they have for the project itself.

"If you're writing cross-genre, it's because you really want to. You're enthusiastic about it, so that enthusiasm comes through," Lallo says. "You can make up for other shortcomings by … being abundantly clear on the page that you had a blast writing it."

STEP 5: TAKE THE RISK

At first glance, Sci-Fi and Westerns seem like two genres that wouldn't go well together. They're entirely different concepts. Yet Space Westerns have become a genre in their own right, hallmarked by stories such as *Star Trek*, *Firefly*, and *Star Wars*.

The idea is so profitable that Disney has built an entire theme park around the concept. But for this to happen, someone had to step out and take the risk—and that individual was C.L. Moore, one of the first creators of a Space Western hero. Moore's character in Northwest Smith made his debut in the 1930s, but it took nearly ninety years from the conception of the idea for Space Westerns to grow to the popularity they enjoy today.

It's completely possible you could write the first book in a brand-new genre and be the founder of a category people didn't even know they wanted. Lallo wants authors to know that if this is your true desire, it is no small undertaking.

"Creating a new niche is like creating a new language," Lallo says. "You have to fully define everything about your story. Everything has to be laid out for the reader."

Overall, writing cross-genre can be an adventure in itself. Despite the challenges writing cross-genre provides, Lallo wouldn't have it any other way. "Writing cross-genre can be an uphill battle, but you're putting out something unique, and that's why we started writing. It keeps you enthusiastic and keeps your mind on fresh ground. It's a rewarding path through the publishing world." ■

Megan Linski-Fox

Marketing 101

READY TO BOOST YOUR BOOK SALES? SCHOOL'S IN SESSION

It's back to school time for the kids, but they aren't the only ones who'll be in class. This month, we're reviewing a few marketing basics and giving you some homework of your own.

LESSON ONE: MAKE IT THE BEST BOOK POSSIBLE

Hopefully, your book is written, edited, and polished to a high shine already. But you can do a few other things to ensure it has a better chance of selling.

Ask a professional to look over your back cover copy. Or if that's not in the budget, run it past some authors in your genre. Get some feedback, and polish that blurb as much as possible.

Take a look at your cover and ensure it's high quality, fits your genre, and easily as visible in miniature on Amazon and other online stores. If it doesn't meet these requirements, you may need a cover revamp.

Evaluate your categories. You can only choose two categories when you set your book up on KDP, but if you message Amazon, you can select up to ten categories. Pick your categories carefully, and think about where best to list your book. Sign into Kindle Direct Publishing

(KDP), then go to Amazon's Contact page: https://author.amazon.com/en_US/contact. Next, select "Amazon Book Page" under "How Can We Help?" and choose "Update Amazon Categories." You can then ask Amazon to add your book to more categories and to remove any existing categories that don't fit your book.

Check your keywords. Dave Chesson of Kindlepreneur has a helpful article on how best to use your keywords: https://kindlepreneur.com/7-kindle-keywords/.

Homework assignment: Before your next book release, go through the above checklist and see how your book measures up.

LESSON TWO: MAKE A PLAN

It really does help to be organized.

Pick your launch date and work backward from there to where you are now.

Put any events on your calendar, such as your book launch party, author takeovers, book signings, and similar events.

Work out when you need to finish graphics, when your book cover will be ready to share, when you're going to email your list, and any other key dates. You could either add your dates to a planner or use an online calendar, whichever works for you.

Set up your social posts in advance with a scheduler like HootSuite or MeetEdgar. That way, you don't have to spend all day constantly posting when you're busy with your launch.

Book promotion sites well in advance. More popular sites fill up quickly, so if you want to book a promo site or two or try promo stacking before your book launch, you will need to plan ahead so that you don't miss out on the promo dates you want.

Homework assignment: Schedule your next launch.

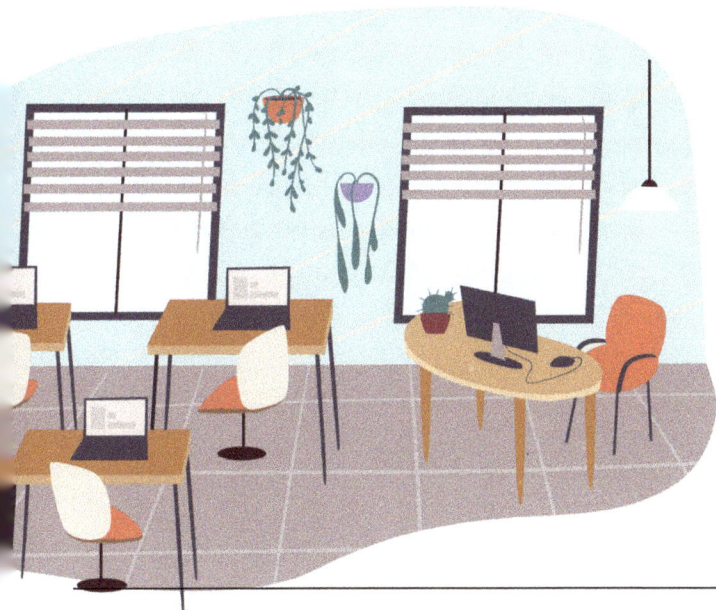

LESSON THREE: BUILD YOUR MAILING LIST

Your mailing list is one of the most important ways you can reach readers who have already shown an interest in your books.

Amazon doesn't give you the contact details of anyone who bought from you, so you have no way of reaching these readers when you release a new book.

If you build your own list, however, you can market to your subscribers whenever you want. And if that marketing is done well, it will get you sales.

The other argument for taking the time to build your mailing list is that if Facebook and other sites kicked you off or suddenly ceased to exist, you wouldn't have any way of reaching your readers. All that time you spent getting likes and followers would be gone, and you wouldn't be able to market your books to those audiences. Without a mailing list, you're vulnerable. With a mailing list, you own a valuable asset that can bring in repeat sales. And it's yours indefinitely.

Homework assignment: Find a solid email platform, and set up your list and a sign-up form on your website. Create a reader magnet and start advertising to your audience.

LESSON FOUR: GET TO KNOW OTHER AUTHORS

Get to know other authors in your genre. Find your tribe, as they say.

Other authors know the utter joy of writing that perfect sentence or how it feels when the words just won't come. They know that writing books is a real job and that indie publishing is just as valid as traditional publishing.

Gather some great author friends around you, and you'll have a team of supportive people who believe in you and who will be there to push you or prop you up when you need it.

When it comes to marketing, you'll find that most author friends will be happy to share your new release in their groups, to share your post, or to give you a like and a comment. You may even be able to arrange newsletter swaps and other promotions between yourselves to get word of your books out there.

Homework assignment: Join at least two genre groups on Facebook. Get to know some authors!

LESSON SIX: DON'T FORGET SEO

Although search engine optimization (SEO) isn't at the top of most book-marketing lists, it does work to get you found in search engine listings.

Take the time to research keywords that you want to be associated with. Then, include them whenever you write.

Use keywords in your social media posts. Add them to your blog posts and your website. Incorporate them in your headers, subheadings, the first paragraph of any copy, in your meta description, in image descriptions, and at least once more in the body of your copy. Don't overdo it and "keyword stuff," but at least do the minimum.

In addition, ensure your website is fast loading and mobile responsive. Both of these are ranking factors for Google results, and they do make a difference. So many people now shop on their phones that you can't afford to have a site that doesn't work on mobile devices. As for site speed, how many seconds will you sit and wait while a site tries to load before you go elsewhere? Probably not long, and your potential readers won't wait forever either.

Homework assignment: Make sure your website is up to date, and start incorporating keywords. Backlinko has a comprehensive Google SEO guide if you're not sure where to start: https://backlinko. com/google-seo-guide.

LESSON FIVE: READ BOOKS IN YOUR GENRE

Reading is priceless research, and it will help you write books that fans of your genre want to read.

Hopefully, you'll be reading something you enjoy, but at the same time, you're also becoming more familiar with your genre, the tropes, and expectations. You're getting to know what your readers want and what makes a great book in your genre.

Homework assignment: Read the top-selling book in your genre. Look at the cover and the blurb too. What can you learn from it? Apply what you've learned to your books.

LESSON SEVEN: REGULARLY CHECK WHAT'S WORKING AND WHAT ISN'T

Not everything you try will work. Keep an eye on your statistics so you can see if your marketing efforts are effective. If you don't check your statistics, you won't know if you're wasting time on what isn't working or not doing enough of what is.

Look at metrics, such as the number of copies sold, number of new email subscribers, clicks and open rates, how much you've earned this month, your monthly word count, or results from using promotional sites. What you choose to measure depends on what is most important to you and how you define success, so decide those first, then pick your metrics.

Check your statistics at the same time each month to see where your readers are coming from, what keywords they are using, and what they're buying. You can then compare your current statistics with last month's to make sure you're moving in the direction you want to go.

And if you're not, regroup and try something new.

Homework assignment: Look at Google analytics for your website, and check your stats on social platforms too. If you've never done it before, you might be in for some surprises.

Book marketing isn't fixed. New ideas and updates constantly crop up. Keep learning and keep up with the latest developments. Lessons don't stop outside the classroom, and that new strategy might lead you and your books to a whole new audience. ■

Gill Fernley

Which Serial Platform Is Right for You?

Authors can publish their stories in many different ways beyond an entire novel released on a certain date. Serial platforms, websites where authors can release stories by episode or chapter instead of as a complete collection, are a great way for authors to gain exposure from readers and get feedback from their audience as they write.

Authors interested in writing and publishing serial fiction have several options when it comes to the distribution of their work. Whether you're most interested in a paying platform, one that offers plenty of customization, or one that allows you to republish your work as a complete collection once it's finished, there is a platform for you.

SUBSTACK

Substack is an online platform that allows users to create subscription-based email newsletters. Authors can use this site to send out monthly emails with a new episode of a story every month. Writers like Fantasy author Maggie Stiefvater have used Substack in the past to share short stories and other small works with readers. The platform is free to use, and authors can publish text and audio without paying for extra storage. Posts can be made free to read or require a paid subscription.

Substack has begun offering new tools to help publishers have more flexibility on the platform as well, such as

- writer profiles: Substack is offering new profiles that make it easier for authors to share their work. Author profiles will show your publications, other Substacks you read, and feeds you've written.
- flexible paywalls: This gives writers control over how much of a paid post they are willing to show as a preview for non-paying readers.
- file embeds: Authors can embed PDFs, Excel spreadsheets, and comic files into their feed, as well as change the title, description, and image of the file. The files will show as a downloadable attachment within the newsletter.

When it comes to posting on Substack, publishers can publish three types of posts: text-based, discussion threads, and podcasts or audio posts. These different types of posts can help publishers reach new audiences and gain a feel for different media types for telling their stories.

When posting on Substack, the following tips can help authors succeed with their newsletters:

- Pick a short and simple title.
- Take advantage of the button feature on your newsletters.
- Take advantage of the different text styles.
- Use hyperlinks.
- Create an online community by interacting with readers.

Substack offers many tools, but a great one is the upgrade option. Once you create an account, you can upgrade your themes to customize your welcome page, the home page, and post by selecting accent colors, font styles, and one of two home page layouts.

PATREON

Patreon is a membership-based platform that allows creators to earn a monthly income by providing rewards and perks for their subscribers. Patreon creators can choose whether to charge per month or per creation (https://support.patreon.com).

Author and Patreon user Miya Kressin says she enjoys Patreon because it's a way for her to talk directly to her readers.

"Patreon is a platform for multiple different artist groups," Kressin says. "For the most part, it allows you to reach out directly to your fans and supporters, and as an author, I use it to allow my readers to come to me to choose what stories they want me to write."

Kressin says she can get to know her readers and what they're like through Patreon's Discord tool. The Discord tool allows her and her supporters to talk in a live room.

"I'll say, 'Hey, find me on Discord. I'm gonna have my camera up. You can talk to me while I'm working on a book cover.' And we'll just sit there and visit while I'm working and put on music and just hang out together," Kressin says.

Kressin has five different tiers on her Patreon. Each tier offers readers increased access and privileges. For example, the one-dollar tier offers early access to her content and access to her cover reveals, and patrons can post about her writing.

Patreon offers many perks for authors, but it also has some drawbacks compared with similar services. Although authors face no upfront costs for using the site, Patreon does take a percentage of the author's funds from their monthly earnings and charges up to 5 percent in credit card processing fees. Still, with the potential to earn a monthly income from content shared across different tiers, it's worth considering as a serial platform, albeit a less conventional one.

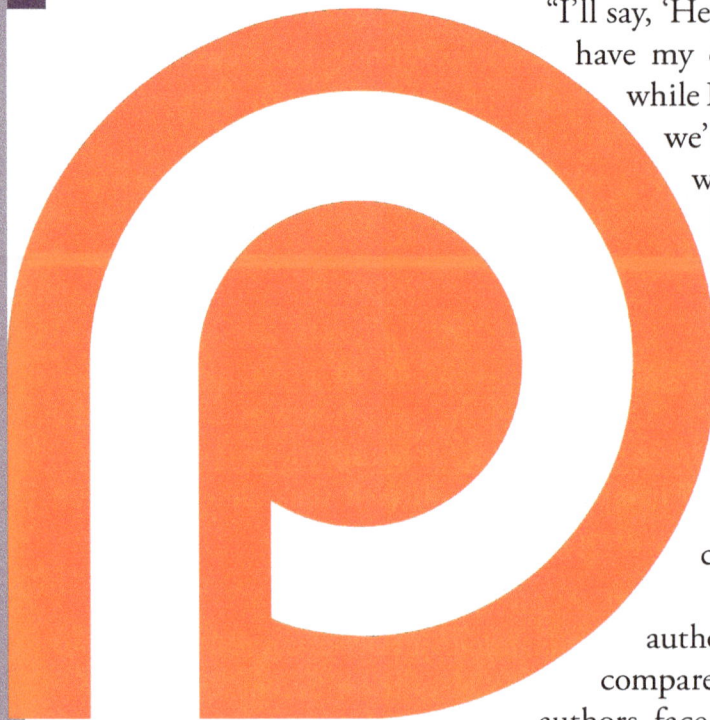

KINDLE VELLA

Kindle Vella (https://amazon.com/kindle-vella) is a relatively new serial platform that launched on Amazon in June 2021. Stories are posted one episode at a time. On Kindle Vella, readers can find detailed story pages for free and access features like "faves" and "thumbs up" awards, which allow readers to engage with stories.

Readers access episodes on Vella with virtual tokens. A full story is five thousand words and costs fifty tokens. A two thousand-word story costs twenty tokens. Tokens are purchased on the site, and authors receive 50 percent of the money spent on tokens paid for their story. If a reader spends $1.99 to purchase two hundred tokens, then spends fifty of them on your full story, you receive twenty-five cents.

Kindle Vella provides a lot of flexibility for authors through the platform. A finished story is not exclusive to the site, so you can repackage it as a book once you are done. Authors can also publish their stories on other serialization platforms, and readers on the site have the opportunity to provide authors with feedback on published episodes.

The platform currently offers fiction in genres such as Action and Adventure, Children's stories, Dystopian, Humor, and more.

WATTPAD

Wattpad is an online-reading platform that's meant for authors to write original stories. Wattpad is based on interaction between readers and authors and gives readers the chance to give feedback to authors.

Wattpad is free to authors and users with no option to sell anything on the platform. This means authors are giving their work away for free. However, Wattpad allows readers to offer immediate feedback on your stories as you write. A comment section also lets readers note what they like and dislike as they read.

When it comes to genres on Wattpad, there is no limit. The site offers more than twenty base genres to help authors categorize their stories, including everything from Romance and Horror to short stories, Vampire fiction, and Fan Fiction. Authors can visit https://support.wattpad.com to view a complete list of base genres.

Pro Tip: When it comes to writing on Wattpad, tailor your content to your selected audience. Write about something well-known to your audience: celebrities, movies, or characters you love. But make sure whatever you write is appealing to your audience. The most important aspect of writing on Wattpad is to make your audience feel special, so interact with them as much as possible.

Finding which serial platform best fits you and your niche doesn't need to be difficult. You will find the right one to help you put your stories out there and that will feel like a perfect match. ∎

Natalie Hobbs

Design like a Pro for free

Tech Tools

Courtesy of IndieAuthorTools.com
Got a tool you love and want to share with us?
Submit a tool at IndieAuthorTools.com

Author Ads Intensive

This course, created by best-selling romance author Skye Warren, "will give you the tools to create Facebook ads that find NEW readers and build an audience that will support your career for years." The material takes you from creation of a profitable ad to scaling those ads and taking control of your career.
https://www.authoradsintensive.com/

K-lytics

"You need market intelligence to invest your time, creativity and money into book market segments and niches that provide the biggest opportunity at the lowest investment," says K-lytics founder Alex Newton. "K-lytics provides you with all the answers you need." The market intelligence service's insights on the Kindle Store are available through monthly subscription or individually priced niche reports.
https://k-lytics.com/

Google Forms

It's easy to create and share online forms and surveys with Google Forms. Just select from multiple question types. Then drag and drop to reorder questions and customize values as easily as pasting in a list. You're also able to analyze responses in real-time. Free for personal use; $12 per user, per month for businesses.
https://www.google.com/forms/

Kindletrends

Kindletrends is a weekly market research newsletter that tells you what's trending in Amazon's Kindle Store. Every week, genre fiction writer Nat Connors compiles a data-rich report on major categories. The service costs $15 per month, with the first month free.
https://kindletrends.com/

Loop11

Test the usability of your website with Loop 11. This user experience testing platform lets you study user intent, test your site's information architecture, and examine user experience changes based on the device they're using. This tool is useful for market research because you can learn if your target consumers find your site easy to navigate and identify issues that prevent conversions.
https://www.loop11.com/

The Transformative Power of Transmedia Storytelling

In 2019, actor Henry Cavill brought monster slayer Geralt of Rivia to life in the series adaptation of *The Witcher* on Netflix. Thus, a new segment of fans was introduced to the elements of Andrzej Sapkowski's world from the novels: the Continent, its fantastical monsters, and its beloved characters.

Originally begun as short stories in his native Poland, Sapkowski expanded and released his five-book Witcher Saga in Polish over a five-year period from 1995 to 1999, with English translations released from 2008 to 2017. The *Witcher* fandom in his native Poland and eastern Europe is often described as cult-like in their appreciation of his work.

Novels were just the beginning. Comic books, video games, role-playing games, and animated shorts were developed, expanding the global fanbase. Other authors followed with spinoffs in cooperation with Sapkowski as a means to keep his fans engaged. These short stories featured familiar characters as well as new ones. Meanwhile, the original stories were translated into multiple languages and adapted into a movie in 2001 and a television series in 2002.

Sapkowski's work and career is just one recent example of the power of transmedia, a method of using a variety of platforms and mediums to expand upon an original story. For indie authors, the practice offers a creative, versatile way to broaden your readership and grow your business—if you know how to use it.

THE CAPITOL

FOR THE CITIZENS
BY THE CAPITOL.

PANEM TODAY.
PANEM TOMORROW.
PANEM FOREVER.

CAPITOL CONCERNS

ONE PANEM

CAPITOL.TV

DISTRICT HEROES

CAPITOL.TV
BROADCAST

President Snow's
Panem Address:
Together as One

WATCH NOW

TRANSMEDIA VERSUS ADAPTATION

You'd be forgiven if you heard the word "transmedia" and didn't immediately understand the term or how it relates to an indie author. You'd also be forgiven if you conflate transmedia with adaptations.

An adaptation takes an existing work and translates it into a different format, such as a movie, graphic novel, translation, or audiobook. The substance of the work remains essentially the same.

Transmedia, on the other hand, makes use of other media. Fantasy and Science Fiction author Jim Wilbourne says, "Transmedia is taking a core story or core world that your story is built in and then expanding it into different types of media so that different readers or different viewers can experience your world but a different story or experience within that world."

For example, in *The Witcher*, adaptations are different versions of the original work—translations from Polish to English, audiobooks, movies, and both television series. Transmedia, on the other hand, are new works—graphic novels, animated shorts, video games, board games, and LitRPG.

You'll likely recognize many mainstream examples of transmedia from pop culture and well-known entertainment franchises:

Pokemon successfully used card games to engage their fandom, which evolved into smartphone apps connecting users globally.

Neil Gaiman's *The Sandman*, recently released as a Netflix series, produced a companion "Dreamcast" on Spotify—a collection of podcast episodes introducing the characters and the land of Dreaming. Gaiman also narrates a bedtime story bound to give you nightmares.

The creators of *The Hunger Games* movie created short videos for YouTube, produced as if sanctioned by Capitol TV and featuring actors describing the different Districts.

The creative team at Watson built two interactive websites for the Hunger Games franchise, one as if it were managed by the oppressive government of the Capitol and another that replaced it during the marketing campaign of the final movie, depicting a takeover by Katniss Everdeen's resistance.

Although these are major mainstream media examples, indie authors can use transmedia to their advantage as well. Urban Fantasy author E.G. Bateman created https://cornerdown.com, which serves to sell branded merchandise and showcase the whimsical Fae menu from her Faders series of books, with a review of the diner from a patron.

Cozy writer Penelope Cress created a church bulletin for her main character's workplace filled with Easter eggs for the next story and included it in her newsletter and on her website. Authors could create a website depicting other elements from their world—for example, the town where a series is set.

EAST COAST VERSUS WEST COAST TRANSMEDIA

Within transmedia, two schools of thought exist as to how the content should be used, commonly referred to as "East Coast" and "West Coast."

Wilbourne prefers to refer to them as going wide versus going deep. Wide, or West Coast, transmedia takes core work and creates new works based in the world. These could include adaptations but also new stories in different forms—animations, web stories, short videos, audiobooks, podcasts, and other mediums. They are both new stories and new methods of delivering those stories.

"Tasty food, set inside another dimension."

It was an real incredible experience for me. The quality of food was only matched by the quality of service I got. I wish I could keep the flavor in my mouth for ever. Thanks for making the evening an unforgettable one.

DREAD LORD MONAMON

Think of a hub and spoke. The hub is the original work with its own set of fans. The spokes are new works in other forms of media, each with its own fans. They may or may not be aware of the other types of work. Some will enter the fandom and learn of the other mediums and become superfans. Others, like video game players, might stay within a single medium.

The deep, or East Coast approach, "[drills] down deeper and deeper for people who love that property already," Willbourne explains. One example he shares is from *The Office*, whose creators filmed a YouTube video with the actors having a simulated everyday conversation in the accounting department.

Other examples could include artwork or podcast interviews with characters. Cozy authors often include recipes, complete cookbooks, or companion social media groups for recipe swaps.

"West Coast and going wide is about attracting different types of people to the property," Wilbourne says. "East Coast is more about deepening relationships."

STARTING ON THE RIGHT FOOT

Indie authors have the benefit of owning their own intellectual property and licensing it as they see fit. If an indie author shares their world and invites other authors to write in it, control still rests with the original author. They retain control as it's an extension of their work rather than an adaptation.

Wilbourne says to approach adaptations and transmedia with the mindset that you're a licensing company. "When you create an audiobook, or if you happen to sell your rights to your book, the company creates an audiobook. You have licensed that property to them. You have not given them the copyright of that. From the very beginning, you're licensing, especially if you do anything outside of just purely writing a book and distributing it yourself."

As with all things, an indie author has to also calculate the return on investment if they want to produce additional creative works. Everything takes time and money to build and maintain, and authors will often need to hire other creatives for ambitious projects.

As you evaluate whether to create transmedia, consider surveying readers if you have an active fandom to see what they'd like. Remember, if you're going wide with transmedia, you're looking to attract new fans that may not know about your books at all and might only be attracted to the app, game, or graphic novel you're creating.

Authors can often get caught up in the excitement of producing more without calculating the return on investment. Wilbourne suggests recouping your investment by including those assets in a Kickstarter or Patreon campaign. You can include different projects at different levels so that you will only need to pay to have them created if the campaign is funded.

WAYS TO START SMALL

When it comes to creating transmedia for your existing works, you're only limited by your imagination and budget. Here are a few ways you can get started with transmedia.

Romance authors can create a series of letters to and from the main characters, set before or after their story.

Create sound file narration and upload to podcast channels.

Fantasy authors can create a board game or dice featuring their characters.

Sports Romance authors can create a website for the fictitious team in their story.

Create printed maps for the world you've created.

Keep in mind that your goal is to delight and engage fans. Whether you go big or start small, your success will depend on ensuring you keep that in mind. "The relationship you build with your readers is invaluable," Wilbourne says. "And building that relationship with your reader is something more valuable than your next sale because they will go out and buy everything from you if you can create that really close bond."

Chelle Honiker

Podcasts We Love

TikTok Marketing Podcast
https://podcasts.apple.com/us/podcast/tiktok-marketing-podcast/id1523057898

Wondering how you can use TikTok to promote your brand? Take a deep dive into organic TikTok marketing strategies and paid TikTok advertising campaigns with hosts Sam Kaufman and Joel Lowinger. The two founded TikTalkMarketingAgency.com, the only agency devoted entirely to marketing on the popular platform. The agency's TikTok Marketing Podcast airs on Thursdays.

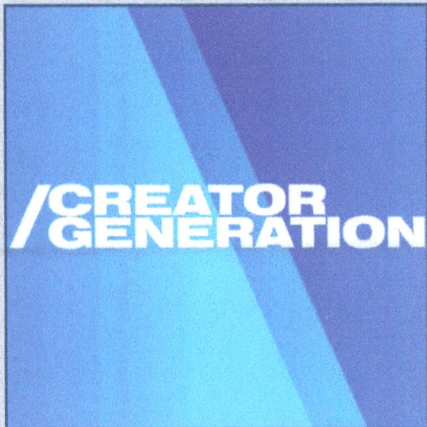

Creator Generation
https://podcasts.apple.com/us/podcast/creator-generation/id1467880508

Want to gain traction with your video content? Check out Creator Generation from Changer Studios. This weekly podcast features "top online video creators and experts sharing their tips, insights and stories for working on YouTube, TikTok and the world's biggest video platforms."

Digital Marketing Podcast
https://podcasts.apple.com/us/podcast/the-digital-marketing-podcast/id373596600

Level up your digital marketing with interviews of experts, the latest industry news, tools, and techniques. This weekly podcast is an ad-free show that strives to be entertaining as well as informative. It's hosted by author Daniel Rowles and marketing expert Ciaran Rogers.

Oh, the Places You'll (Virtually) Go

WHILE YOUR CHARACTERS TRAVEL THE WORLD, ADD REAL DETAILS WITH THE WORLD WIDE WEB

When it comes to choosing a location for a novel, short story, or script, many authors stick with what they know. Stephen King's novels typically stay in Maine. Hailing from Kansas City, Missouri, Gillian Flynn's three novels take place in the rural Midwest. Anne Rice is well known for her exotic paranormal tales, which mostly take place in her hometown of New Orleans.

Mystery and Thriller author Leila Kirkconnell sticks with the places she knows from various parts of the United States. "Even though my stories take place in different cities, they are all where I have been," she writes. "Writing what I know helps me with authenticity, and it's nice having my characters walk where I have previously been. Going back to those cities, I can watch my stories unfold in my mind."

Sometimes, a story calls for a different backdrop, quite possibly in a location where the author has never visited. When this happens, you can make your work as genuine as possible by adding locations and landmarks as well as capturing the overall feel of the area without insulting the residents.

The obvious way to familiarize oneself with a new city or town is to plan a visit, but even if you're setting your story in a location where you went once for vacation, you will need to supplement that with research. What you see on a weekend trip is not what the general population of that city sees. You will need to mingle with locals, find the out-of-the-way places that only residents know about, sample the local cuisine, and ensure you represent the area accurately.

Pro Tip: Safety comes first, so ensure that you aren't headed to an area that's high in crime or that's unsafe for out-of-towners. Research your destination thoroughly beforehand to ensure you are safe at all times.

Traveling to a location isn't always possible, however. In this case, research is paramount to setting your book in an unknown location, but accurately representing that area can still be challenging. Just Googling a city and reading about it is usually not enough. You will need to dig deeper. Watch videos about the area, join a locals group on Facebook, or interview those who live there. Utilize Google Earth to "visit" the area. Flickr also has pictures of just about anywhere in the world.

While writing, pay attention to terrain and landmarks, and study up on the climate and anything unusual in the area. If you set your book in Alaska during polar night, you wouldn't want to write about sunshine-filled days. Look up weather patterns so you know if the area has a rainy season, a time when it's particularly windy, and how much snow is typical. The Farmers' Almanac (https://farmersalmanac.com) is an amazing resource for future weather forecasts for a region, but it also provides information, such as a full-moon calendar, a zodiac calendar, and hunting and fishing calendars.

Pro Tip: *The Urban Setting Thesaurus* and *The Rural Setting Thesaurus* from Writers Helping Writers provide incredible detail and information about more than one hundred settings, including details that will help you elevate your writing with "show, don't tell."

Each area in the world also has language differences, not only in accents but also in the way they say certain words or phrases. If you use "pop" in an area where they say "soda," readers in the region will know you are unfamiliar with their way of life. As for accents, even traveling forty-five minutes in a different direction can result in different speech patterns. Search for videos from the area so you know how to write dialect, but remember that even people within the same region might have different accents.

Reading books by authors who are from the area can help you incorporate accurate information into your story, and watching movies about a location can provide a great visual aid. Try indie films first, as those are often filmed in the same region where the story takes place.

If you're writing anything to do with crime, research local city, county, and state regulations, penal codes, and sentencing guidelines. Police department sites often have statistics on crime, but if they don't, several websites track local stats and recent crimes, such as Crime-Mapping (https://crimemapping.com) and the FBI website (https://fbi.gov/services/cjis/ucr) in the US. For smaller or rural locations, you may need to contact the local police or sheriff's department to glean that information.

Authors writing Historical Fiction can watch documentaries or videos from that time frame if possible. If you can, interview people who lived in that area during that period. Otherwise, seek out legitimate resources, such as textbooks, newspapers, or firsthand accounts. Books written in that time period may help too.

Authors Marisa Oldham and Carraine Oldham wrote about Nazi-occupied Poland in their book, *Remember the Stars*. "For over a month, we watched every Holocaust documentary we could, for not only the history but to better describe the location we were writing," Marisa Oldham says.

"With our topic of the Holocaust, it was important more than ever for us to describe everything exactly as it was," Carraine Oldham says. "We learned so much about what it looked like in that time period, and it helped us to enter a past world, which would have been impossible without hours upon hours of research."

Anyone can set their story in an area with which they are unfamiliar, even if you cannot visit in person. With a lot of dedication and research, you can make a world come alive so that you even impress the locals. ■

Angie Martin

The Superhero's Secret, Revealed

From the golden age of comics to modern-day Marvel movies, countless caped crusaders and super villains have kept our pulses pounding with their daring and dastardly deeds, leaving us breathless and clamoring for more.

Traditionally, Superhero fiction has been a visual medium, so unsurprisingly, fans often gravitate toward comics, movies, cartoons, or games for its stories. However, both graphic and longer-form novels are an important part of the genre that shouldn't be overlooked. It would be easy to do, as this popular class of Sci-Fi story can sometimes fly under the radar in the literary world, crossing genres into areas such as Action, Contemporary, or even Romance. Yet that versatility can be its own superpower, appealing to a variety of readers from countless backgrounds even as the genre's popularity grows on its own.

Ask any superhero fan which authors or artists have created the most enduring characters in the genre, and almost everyone's list will include a few of the greats: Stan Lee and Jack Kirby, or Jerry Siegel and Joe Shuster. Yet ask those same fans to tell you what drew them to their stories, and you might be surprised at how different their answers are.

An astounding volume of comics, books, films, and other superhero stories spans a history of more

A LOOK AT THE TROPES THAT MAKE THE GENRE SOAR

than eighty years. The list of tropes related to the superhero genre stretches almost as long as Rubberband Man, and everyone has their own preference for what makes a story stand out. However, all superhero tales have certain key tropes in common.

ORIGIN STORY

Author Shannon Alder once said, "Heroes are not made. They are born out of circumstances and rise to the occasion when their spirit can no longer coexist with the hypocrisy of injustice to others."

Superman's parents sent him to earth to avoid the cataclysm that destroyed Krypton. Batman sought to avenge his parent's murder. Morbius was looking to cure his blood disease. Your character's origin story sets the stage for how and why they became super in the first place, and it ranks high on the list of tropes you should consider when crafting a superhero tale.

TEAM-UP STORY

A great hero tale doesn't always need to start at the beginning. Some of the best stories in the genre are a result of two or more heroes teaming up to save our imperiled world from impending doom or ultimate destruction. Think Sub-Mariner and the Human Torch putting aside their rivalry and joining forces.

SECRET IDENTITIES

Peter Parker is a bespectacled freelance photographer by day and a web-slinging superhero by night. Bruce Wayne is an uber-wealthy, suit-wearing business mogul one minute and a latex-wrapped crusader for justice the next.

Among the most frequently encountered tropes is a secret identity, followed by the lengths our hero must go to conceal it. Within the genre, this has given rise to the use of special suits or costumes that do everything from concealing heroes' identities to providing them with the enhanced abilities in the first place.

EQUALLY MATCHED COUNTERPART

When crafting your super villains, both their motivation and their powers should be an even match for your hero as they are the main source of conflict for your story. Too little conflict can lead to boredom, and too much conflict can stifle your hero's growth.

Just as your hero must have a motivation for taking up the cape, their foe must also have a raison d'être. Bad guys are never bad just for the fun of it—they, too, need a compelling reason to wreak havoc.

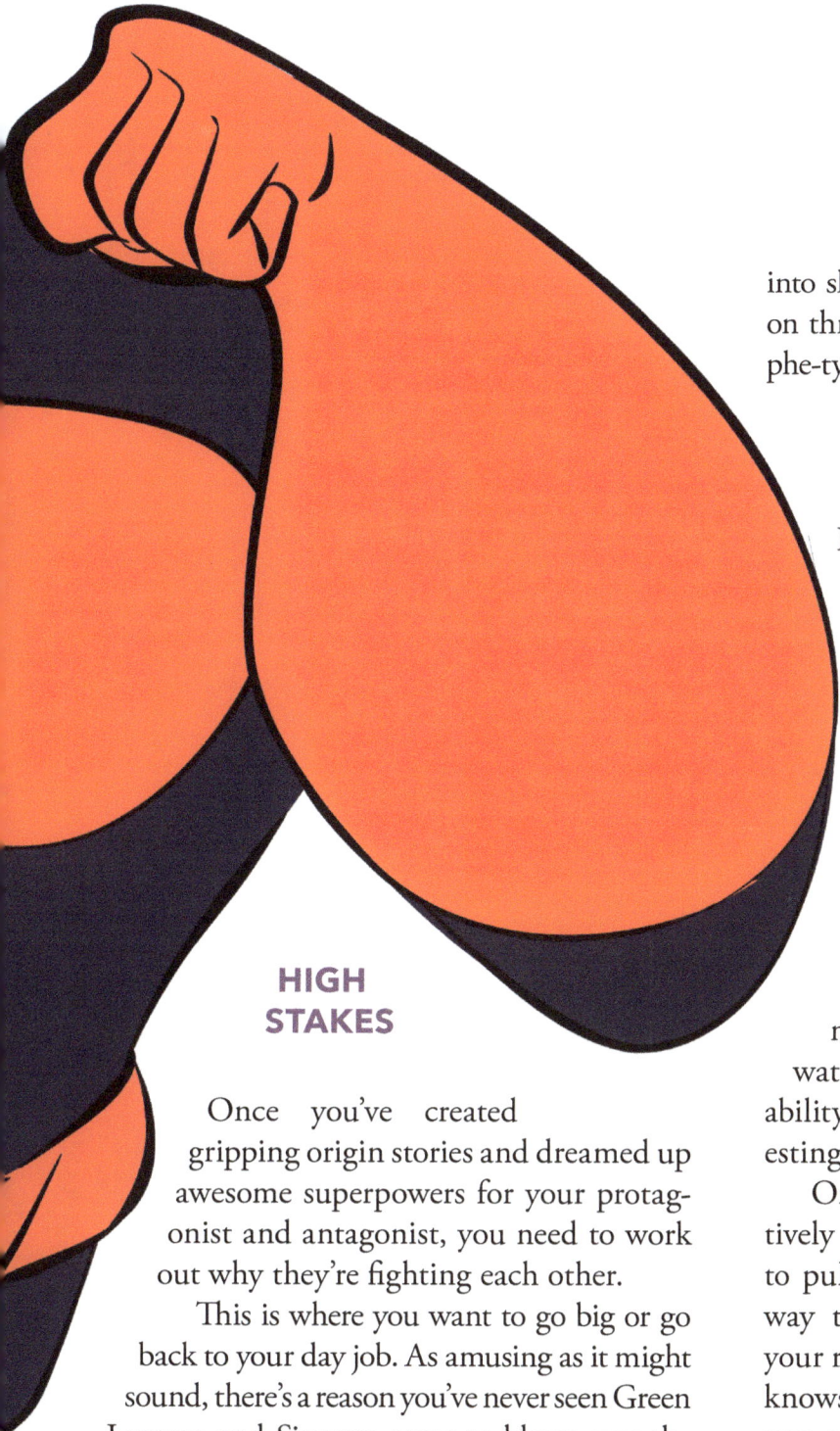

into skin-tight spandex, you'd better be planning on throwing some life-and-death, major-catastrophe-type situations on the page.

ACHILLES'S HEEL

Last but certainly not least, however super they are, your main character needs a vulnerability. The best characters are multi-dimensional. Creating a hero or a villain that is all-powerful leaves no room for suspense, and let's face it: One of the main reasons we all love a thrilling superhero story is the suspense associated with wondering whether good will triumph over evil.

No matter the weakness—Superman's aversion to kryptonite or Sandman's breakdown when confronted with water or extreme heat—some type of vulnerability will make your characters more interesting and relatable.

Once you have figured out how to effectively use these tropes or marry two or more to pull your readers in, you'll be well on your way to creating Superhero fiction that keeps your readers on the edge of their seats. And who knows? Maybe one day, one of the greats that you so admire in this industry will approach you to work together. ■

Jenn Mitchell

HIGH STAKES

Once you've created gripping origin stories and dreamed up awesome superpowers for your protagonist and antagonist, you need to work out why they're fighting each other.

This is where you want to go big or go back to your day job. As amusing as it might sound, there's a reason you've never seen Green Lantern and Sinestro come to blows over the last dinner roll at Thanksgiving. If you're going to ask your character to don their alter ego and slip

Breathe In, Breathe Out

FOUR WAYS TO STRESS LESS

According to Zippia (https://zippia.com), a job recruiting site, 83 percent of US workers experience work-related stress. But what is stress, and what's the difference between normal stress, burnout, and depression?

Stress is about feeling overwhelmed, as though you have too much on your plate, and according to Psych Central (https://psychcentral.com), it can lead to burnout. Burnout, a feeling of emotional, physical, and mental exhaustion, only tends to affect one aspect of your life, namely work. Depression, although similar, is more pervasive and affects every aspect of your life.

Burnout can lead to depression but not the other way around, according to Psych Central. Still, both can have lasting effects on one's mental health if left untreated, so if you're experiencing symptoms of either, reach out and talk to a trusted friend or family member.

If you've been feeling a bit stressed recently, it's better to nip it in the bud. Here are a few ways to help you survive.

1. **Try meditation.** The Calm App (https://calm. com) is a helpful resource for mindfulness and relaxation techniques. Whether you're struggling with sleep or trying to stay focused, it has plenty of guidance to help you feel in control again.
2. **Journal about what's on your mind.** Sometimes, just a plain old brain dump of everything that's on your mind can help you feel more relaxed and in control—like unbuttoning your pants after a big Thanksgiving meal. The stress comes from trying to control things that we can't control. Write a list of everything on your mind, cross out the things you can't control, and focus on the ones you can.
3. **Take a break.** Give yourself permission to have time off, whether it's the whole day or just an hour or two. It might seem counterintuitive when your to-do list could be a novella, but giving your brain a little space can boost your creativity.
4. **Use Neuro Linguistic Programming (NLP).** This little-known technique is especially helpful if the root of your stress is a problem you've been struggling to solve. Pick any book, fiction or nonfiction, and before you start reading, tell yourself this: "I will find the answer to my problem in this book." Then, start reading, and let your brain work its magic in the background.

Whether you use these techniques or try your own, find an effective way to minimize stress. Your future self will thank you! ∎

Angela Archer

The Silent Struggle
WAYS TO MANAGE MENTAL HEALTH

With one in five Americans dealing with mental health problems, mental well-being is becoming a bigger and more important topic than ever before. Mental illness has been suggested to share a link with creativity, with famed cases such as Edgar Allen Poe, Sylvia Plath, Mark Twain, and Stephen King, and a plethora of scientific evidence and research back up the theory, according to the Writing Cooperative (https://writingco-operative.com).

While the story of the tragic artist becomes almost romanticized in books and movies, it remains a serious issue for those affected. Writing can sometimes provide catharsis, but on days when symptoms make creativity too difficult, you can manage a mental health condition in many ways.

First and foremost, seek professional help. Find a psychiatrist to work with you on medication if necessary, and locate a therapist you are comfortable with—both go a long way in getting your mental health back on track. If you're not comfortable with face-to-face appointments, consider resources for therapists online, such as "Better Help" and "ReGain." The American Psychological Association offers great information on what to look for in a therapist. Some therapists specialize in specific areas of mental health, such as obsessive-compulsive disorder, post-traumatic stress disorder, eating disorders, or others, and finding a professional who works almost exclusively with your diagnosis can help with managing your health.

Beyond seeking assistance, find an activity or event to look forward to. When suffering from depression, for instance, you can easily spiral with debilitating thoughts of worthlessness, and as a creative, any negative reviews can feed that notion. Looking forward to something can ease one's sense of doom. Schedule a trip, a dinner with friends, or a day out with kids or your significant other. Plan to see a movie at the theater or even via a streaming service, although getting out of the house can boost your mood. Caring for plants, spending time in your yard, a walk in the park, or a short trip to the corner store can also assuage your depression. Even the smallest event can be the key to moving from day to day.

Finally, always remember your importance. You are valuable, loved, needed, and wanted. You are beautiful inside and out, and you provide entertainment to others with your talent. Constantly remind yourself of these and other affirmations. Write encouraging notecards to place in your office or your writing area, surround yourself with inspirational sayings that help build self-esteem, and never forget your worth.

This is the second in a series of articles discussing mental illness and the role it can play in an author's career. ◼

Angie Martin

As always, if you suffer from mental illness, these tips are not in lieu of seeking proper professional treatment. If you are in immediate danger and dealing with suicidal thoughts or tendencies, please contact the National Suicide Hotline at 988 or a local hotline. Call 911 to have an ambulance sent to your location, or seek immediate treatment at the closest emergency room. You can also contact NAMI at 800-950-NAMI (6264) or live chat with a professional on the organization's website, https://nami.org.

Behind the Scenes at Self Publishing Show Live

AN SPS VOLUNTEER RECAPS HER TAKEAWAYS FROM THE TWO-DAY EVENT

When Mark Dawson made his clarion call for volunteers to help backstage and front-of-house for the Self Publishing Show Live event, held June 28 and 29 in London's South Bank, I hesitated to raise my hand.

The inaugural event, back in 2020, heralded the start of lockdown, and there was an excellent chance I actually had COVID on the day—I just didn't know it then. I did know, though, that I was so ill that afternoon that I skipped the final talk and left my plans to go to the aftershow party to catch an earlier train home and collapse in my bed.

Two and a bit years later, the team was not only planning another event, but it was to be bigger, better, bolder—well, a day longer, at least. So what's a girl to do? I was determined to make the most of the opportunity this time, so I volunteered to don the yellow T-shirt and dive in.

June appears to be conference season for European indie authors. The SPS conference came hot on the heels of a number of others across the continent, including 20Books events across the United Kingdom as well as in Madrid and Amsterdam. Many travelers arrived at London South Bank after being on the indie author trail for a month or more, but this did not appear to dampen their enthusiasm. Everyone I met over these two days remained hungry for learning and chance conversations. The buzz backstage and in the reception lounge was palpable.

I had requested to be at the registration desk. Squeezed snuggly into my yellow and black worker bee outfit, I joined my teammates in downloading the required booking app and began scanning. Any silly notions I held about being able to sit down on the job evaporated the moment the doors opened. It was like Harrods's Boxing Day sale—or a Black Friday event at Macy's, for my American friends. And the flow of excited, often nervous, but genuinely curious writers remained constant until the show began at nine o'clock.

I valiantly offered, with my wonderful sidekick, Ben, to hang back at our posts for any stragglers. We were an efficient team, attaching name cards to lanyards in between registrations with a deft skill akin to my old grandmother shelling peas over a pan in the backyard.

This meant that I missed the first two sessions, which is a shame because I heard afterward that the first talk was awesome. Fortunately, I made it into the auditorium in time to watch Joanna Penn outline her vision for the future. I am not at liberty in this report to summarize all the amazing AI innovations she showcased, but I can say that I was inspired and overwhelmed in equal measure.

Then came lunch and finally a chance to network properly and talk to my fellow indies. I met many of these amazing people at the 20Books writing retreat and conference in Edinburgh in 2019. Only with fellow self-publishing authors can I completely nerd out about Kindle Unlimited versus wide, discuss the merits of a BookBub deal, or debate the best online courses for Amazon Ads or the merits of plotting versus pantsing.

And discuss all things word counts. Target word counts. Average word counts. Daily word counts.

On a side note, I haven't mentioned yet that it was also my birthday. Yes, I chose to wear yellow and work for free on the anniversary of my entry into this physical plane. And I would do it again in a heartbeat.

But my birthday held one major drawback. I was in London, and my London-based offspring wanted to take me out for dinner. Normally, this would be a wondrous thing, but it meant that I missed my own party. I have heard tales and seen pictures, and it looked like a great time was had by all.

Getting up at four in the morning for the second day in a row was not easy, but I was excited to see what Day Two would bring. This time, I was only required to mill around and look helpful, so I was able to relax more and enjoy the show. It's hard to pick highlights; all the speakers were excellent.

Looking back over my notes, what were my biggest takeaways from the talks?

Joanna Penn said, "You can choose fear or you can choose curiosity," and there is so much to remain curious about. I am terrified of TikTok, but maybe I should, instead, develop a more inquiring mind about this popular platform and engage with BookTokers. I blame James Blatch for that.

Or I should listen to Janet Margot and get over my fear of Amazon Ads. The game is less scary once you know the rules. Follow the ASINs, Amazon's unique product identification numbers.

Suzy K. Quinn made me reconsider what makes a best-selling book. I need a compelling one-sentence premise for my next work in progress and to stop worrying I'm not a good enough writer. Am I a good enough storyteller though?

Above all, from the panel discussions and speakers, I learned the difference between being a writer and being a five-, six-, or seven-figure author is deciding that this is a business. I need to make business decisions, not emotional ones. I need to develop quality products people want and then learn how to deliver them. It's that simple—and that difficult—a task.

When Mark Dawson called the minions up the front for a round of applause, I felt elated to be a small part of the team that had made this show possible. I met or reengaged with wonderful, inspiring people and learned from those who are making it happen. The buzz was infectious—though hopefully this time, coronavirus wasn't.

Would I volunteer again? Totally.

Should you attend an indie author conference if you get the chance? Absolutely.

They really are life-changing. ■

Susan Odev

MERCH FOR AUTHORS

Branded merch on Etsy, Amazon, and your own site.
Learn about extended stock licenses.
Includes sample contracts.

envato elements

Travel & Hotel Email Builder
By theemon

Travel Email Builder
By HyperPix

Kant - Email Template
By ThemeMountain

Olive - Fashion Email Template
By giantdesign

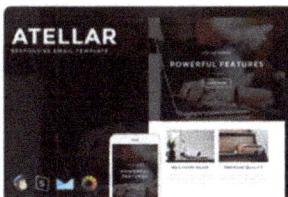

Metro App - Instapage Template
By Morad

ButaPest Email Template
By JeetuG

All the Email Templates you need and many other design elements, are available for a monthly subscription by subscribing to Envato Elements. The subscription costs $16.50 per month and gives you **unlimited access** to a massive and growing library of **1,500,000+** items that can be downloaded as often as you need (stock photos too)!

DOWNLOAD NOW

From the Stacks

Courtesy of IndieAuthorTools.com
Got a book you love and want to share with us?
Submit a book at IndieAuthorTools.com

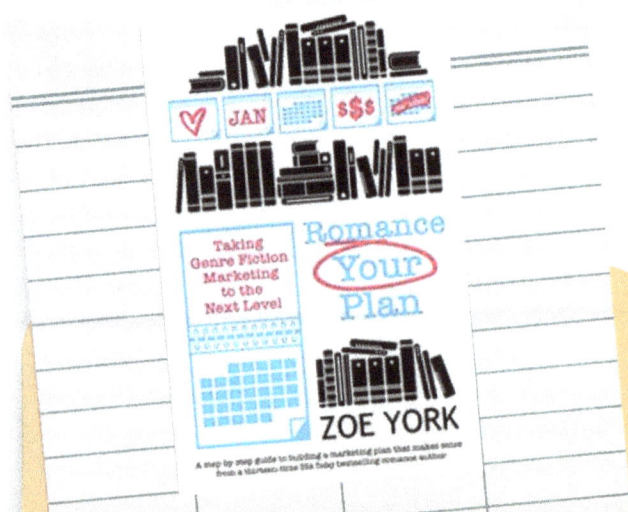

Romance Your Plan: Taking Genre Fiction Marketing to the Next Level

https://books2read.com/u/bP71ZR

In Romance Your Plan, bestselling author Zoe York explores "how to pick the right marketing plan for your brand, your books, and your readers." Discussion topics include planning releases, brand revamping, audience growth, scheduling sales, and goal setting. This is the second book in her Publishing How To series.

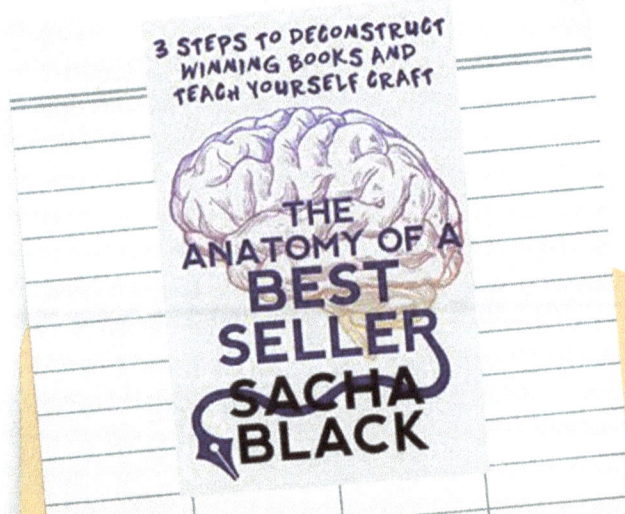

The Anatomy of a Best Seller: 3 Steps to Deconstruct Winning Books and Teach Yourself Craft

https://books2read.com/u/3LVrGD

The Anatomy of a Best Seller "will help you break down the best books in your genre, understand how and why they work, and then learn how to do it yourself." Author Sacha Black's latest addition to her Better Writers series provides "tips and tricks for breaking down everything from sentence level prose to plot, pacing, characters, story arcs, and more."

DATE DUE

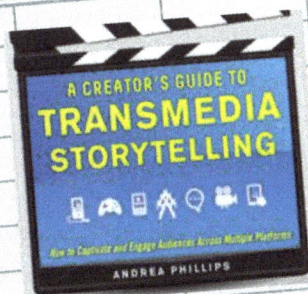

A Creator's Guide to Transmedia Storytelling

https://books2read.com/u/4AvgJK

If you want to attract, engage, and captivate your audience, you need this book. Written by an award-winning transmedia creator and renowned games designer, this book shows you how to utilize the same marketing tools used by heavy-hitters such as HBO, Disney, Ford, and Sony Pictures — at a fraction of the cost.

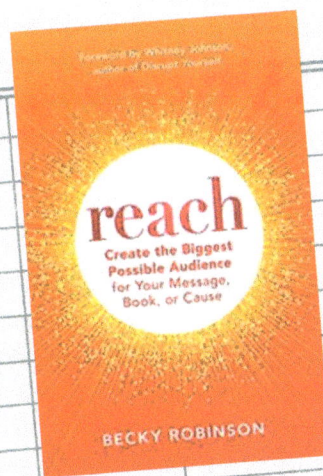

Reach: Create the Biggest Possible Audience for Your Message, Book, or Cause

https://books2read.com/u/m2dXxR

Audiobook

Reach provides a clear and structured approach to creating a successful online presence that will create the biggest possible impact for any message. Becky Robinson shares a framework to cultivate followers that requires four commitments: value, consistency, endurance, and generosity.

Finding the Right Message

https://books2read.com/u/b5jOxk

Jen Havice, messaging strategist and customer-driven copywriter, walks you through how to ask the right questions to learn what makes your customers tick so you can produce copy your visitors can't resist. Filled with examples, templates, and case studies, this second edition of Finding the Right Message is both practical and timely.

In This Issue

Executive Team

Chelle Honiker, Publisher

As the publisher of Indie Author Magazine, Chelle Honiker brings nearly three decades of startup, technology, training, and executive leadership experience to the role. She's a serial entrepreneur, founding and selling multiple successful companies including a training development company, travel agency, website design and hosting firm, a digital marketing consultancy, and a wedding planning firm. She's organized and curated multiple TEDx events and hired to assist other nonprofit organizations as a fractional executive, including The Travel Institute and The Freelance Association.

As a writer, speaker, and trainer she believes in the power of words and their ability to heal, inspire, incite, and motivate. Her greatest inspiration is her daughters, Kelsea and Cathryn, who tolerate her tendency to run away from home to play with her friends around the world for months at a time. It's said she could run a small country with just the contents of her backpack.

Alice Briggs, Creative Director

As the creative director of Indie Author Magazine, Alice Briggs utilizes her more than three decades of artistic exploration and expression, business startup adventures, and leadership skills. A serial entrepreneur, she has started several successful businesses. She brings her experience in creative direction, magazine layout and design, and graphic design in and outside of the indie author community to her role.

With a masters of science in Occupational Therapy, she has a broad skill set and uses it to assist others in achieving their desired goals. As a writer, teacher, healer, and artist, she loves to see people accomplish all they desire. She's excited to see how IAM will encourage many authors to succeed in whatever way they choose. She hopes to meet many of you in various places around the world once her passport is back in use.

Nicole Schroeder, Editor in Chief

Nicole Schroeder is a storyteller at heart. As the editor in chief of Indie Author Magazine, she brings nearly a decade of journalism and editorial experience to the publication, delighting in any opportunity to tell true stories and help others do the same. She holds a bachelor's degree from the Missouri School of Journalism and minors in English and Spanish. Her previous work includes editorial roles at local publications, and she's helped edit and produce numerous fiction and nonfiction books, including a Holocaust survivor's memoir, alongside independent publishers. Her own creative writing has been published in national literary magazines. When she's not at her writing desk, Nicole is usually in the saddle, cuddling her guinea pigs, or spending time with family. She loves any excuse to talk about Marvel movies and considers National Novel Writing Month its own holiday.

Writers

Angela Archer

Having worked as a mental health nurse for many years, Angela combines her love of words with her love of human psychology to work as a copywriter in the UK. She independently published a novella and novel in 2020 and is currently fending off the lure of shiny new novel ideas to complete the second book in her sci-fi series.

When she's not tinkering with words, she's usually drinking tea, playing the saxophone (badly), or being mum and wife to her husband and two boys.

Gill Fernley

Gill Fernley writes fiction in several genres under different pen names, but what all of them have in common is humour and romance, because she can't resist a happy ending or a good laugh. She's also a freelance content writer and has been running her own business since 2013. Before that, she was a technical author and documentation manager for an engineering company and can describe to you more than you'd ever wish to know about airflow and filtration in downflow booths. Still awake? Wow, that's a first! Anyway, that experience taught her how to explain complex things in straightforward language and she hopes it will come in handy for writing articles for IAM. Outside of writing, she's a cake decorator, expert shoe hoarder, and is fluent in English, dry humour and procrastibaking.

Natalie Hobbs

My name is Natalie Hobbs and I am a Journalism major from Houston, TX. I am a senior at Texas Tech University and will be graduating this August. My favorite things to do are spend time with my two dogs and family, cook, and go shopping! After college, I want to work in the influencer marketing field and eventually open up my own non-profit.

Megan Linski-Fox

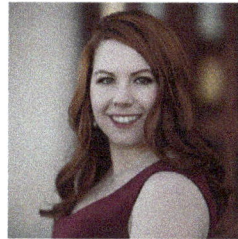

Megan Linski lives in Michigan. She is a USA TODAY Bestselling Author and the author of more than fifty novels. She has over fifteen years of experience writing books alongside working as a journalist and editor. She graduated from the University of Iowa, where she studied Creative Writing.

Megan advocates for the rights of the disabled, and is an activist for mental health awareness. She co-writes the Hidden Legends Universe with Alicia Rades. She also writes under the pen name of Natalie Erin for the Creatures of the Lands series, co-authored by Krisen Lison.

Craig Martelle

High school Valedictorian enlists in the Marine Corps under a guaranteed tank contract. An inauspicious start that was quickly superseded by excelling in language study. Contract waived, a year at the Defense Language Institute to learn Russian and off to keep my ears on the big red machine during the Soviet years. Back to

DLI for advanced Russian after reenlisting. Deploying. Then getting selected to get a commission. Earned a four-year degree in two years by majoring in Russian Language. It was a cop out, but I wanted to get back to the fleet. One summa cum laude graduation later, that's where I found myself. My first gig as a second lieutenant was on a general staff. I did well enough that I stayed at that level or higher for the rest of my career, while getting some choice side gigs – UAE, Bahrain, Korea, Russia, and Ukraine.

Major Martelle. I retired from the Marines after a couple years at the embassy in Moscow working arms control issues. The locals called me The German, because of my accent in Russian. That worked for me. It kept me off the radar. Just until it didn't. Expelled after two years for activities inconsistent with my diplomatic status, I went to Ukraine. Can't let twenty years of Russian language go to waste. More arms control. More diplomatic stuff. Then 9/11 and off to war. That was enough deployment for me. Then came retirement.

Department of Homeland Security was a phenomenally miserable gig. I quit that job quickly enough and went to law school. A second summa cum laude later and I was working for a high-end consulting firm performing business diagnostics, business law, and leadership coaching. More deployments. For the money they paid me, I was good with that. Just until I wasn't. Then I started writing. You'll find Easter eggs from my career hidden within all my books. Enjoy the stories.

Angie Martin

Award-winning author Angie Martin has spent over a decade mentoring and helping new and experienced authors as they prepare to send their babies into the world. She relies on her criminal justice background and knack for researching the tiniest of details to assist others when crafting their own novels. She has given countless speeches in various aspects of writing, including creating characters, self-publishing, and writing supernatural and paranormal. She also assisted in leading a popular California writers' group, which organized several book signings for local authors. In addition to having experience in film, she created the first interactive murder mystery on Clubhouse and writes and directs each episode. Angie now resides in rural Tennessee, where she continues to help authors around the world in every stage of publication while writing her own thriller and horror books, as well as branching out into new genres.

Jenn Mitchell

Jenn Mitchell writes Urban Fantasy and Weird West, as well as culinary cozy mysteries under the pen name, J Lee Mitchell. She writes, cooks, and gardens in the heart of South Central Pennsylvania's Amish Country. When she's not doing these things, she dreams of training llama riding ninjas.

She enjoys traveling, quilting, hoarding cookbooks, Sanntangling, and spending time with the World's most patient and loving significant other.

Susan Odev

Susan has banked over three decades of work experience in the fields of personal and organizational development, being a freelance corporate trainer and consultant alongside holding down "real" jobs for over twenty-five years. Specializing in entrepreneurial mindsets, she has written several non-fiction business books, once gaining a coveted Amazon #1 best seller tag in business and entrepreneurship, an accolade she now strives to emulate with her fiction.

Currently working on her fifth novel, under a top secret pen name, the craft and marketing aspects of being a successful indie author equally fascinate and terrify her.

A lover of history with a criminal record collection, Susan lives in a retro orange and avocado world. Once described by a colleague as being an "onion," Susan has many layers, as have ogres (according to Shrek). She would like to think this makes her cool, her teenage children just think she's embarrassing.

Ready to level up your indie author career?

Trick question. Of course you are.

*INDIE ^Author Tools

Get Your Friday Five Newsletter and find your next favorite tool here.

https://writelink.to/iat

Join the Facebook group here.

https://writelink.to/iatfb

COME VISIT
the *Cake Machine* STAY for the *Conference.*

Las Vegas
Nevada
November
14-18, 2022

writelink.to/20Books

20 BOOKS TO 50K®
A RISING TIDE LIFTS ALL BOATS